☞ W9-AFH-587

Vegetable Timeline

8000–5000 BCE

Potatoes are first grown in Peru.

1000 BCE

Cabbages and kale are grown by the Celts.

2680 BCE

Lettuce is cultivated in Egypt.

ca. 100 BCE

Spinach is first cultivated in what is Iran today.

3500 BCE

Onions, leeks, and garlic are grown in Egypt.

200 BCE

The Romans start to grow asparagus.

2000 BCE

Egyptian temple paintings are created of a purple plant that may be a carrot.

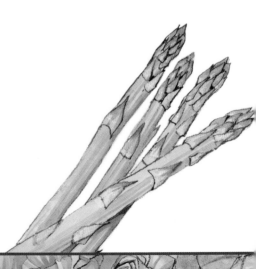

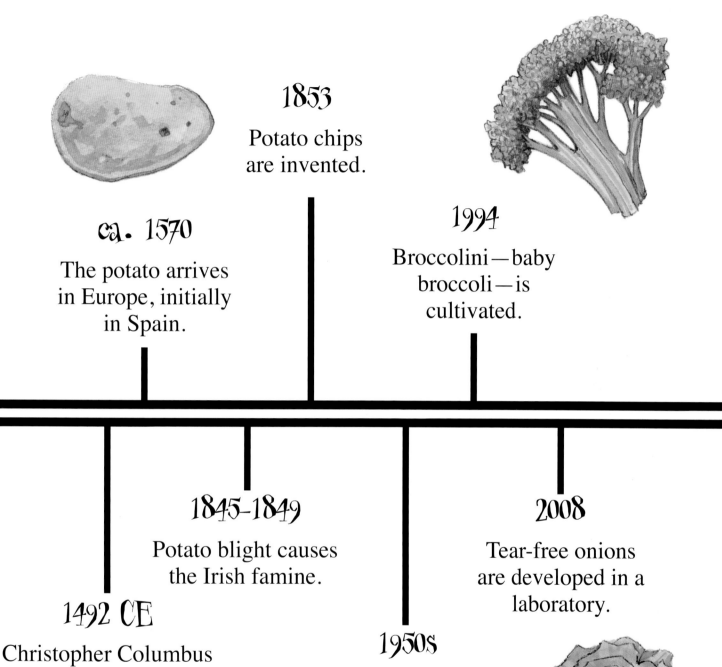

1853
Potato chips are invented.

ca. 1570
The potato arrives in Europe, initially in Spain.

1994
Broccolini—baby broccoli—is cultivated.

1845–1849
Potato blight causes the Irish famine.

2008
Tear-free onions are developed in a laboratory.

1492 CE
Christopher Columbus introduces onions to the Americas.

1950s
Vacuum cooling makes it easier to cool and store lettuce.

Where Vegetables Come From

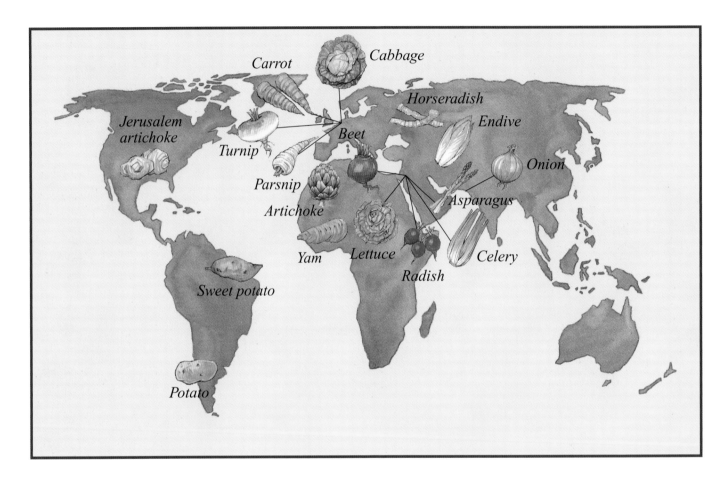

The above map shows the places where many of our most popular vegetables were first cultivated. As can be seen, many of them came from South America, the Middle East, and northern Europe.

Author:

Alex Woolf studied history at Essex University, England. He is the author of over 60 books for children, many of them on historical topics. They include *You Wouldn't Want to Live Without Books!, You Wouldn't Want to Live Without Money!,* and *You Wouldn't Want to Live Without Poop!*

Artist:

David Antram was born in Brighton, England, in 1958. He studied at Eastbourne College of Art and then worked in advertising for 15 years before becoming a full-time artist. He has illustrated many children's nonfiction books.

Series creator:

David Salariya was born in Dundee, Scotland. He has illustrated a wide range of books and has created and designed many new series for publishers in the UK and overseas. David established The Salariya Book Company in 1989. He lives in Brighton with his wife, illustrator Shirley Willis, and their son, Jonathan.

Editor: **Jacqueline Ford**

Editorial Assistant: **Mark Williams**

PAPER FROM
SUSTAINABLE
FORESTS

© The Salariya Book Company Ltd MMXVI
No part of this publication may be reproduced in whole or in part, or stored in a retrieval system, or transmitted in any form or by any means, electronic, mechanical, photocopying, recording, or otherwise, without written permission of the publisher. For information regarding permission, write to the copyright holder.

Published in Great Britain in 2016 by
The Salariya Book Company Ltd
25 Marlborough Place, Brighton BN1 1UB

ISBN-13: 978-0-531-21490-9 (lib. bdg.) 978-0-531-22440-3 (pbk.)

All rights reserved.
Published in 2016 in the United States
by Franklin Watts
An imprint of Scholastic Inc.

A CIP catalog record for this book is available
from the Library of Congress.

Printed and bound in China.
Printed on paper from sustainable sources.
1 2 3 4 5 6 7 8 9 10 R 25 24 23 22 21 20 19 18 17 16

SCHOLASTIC, FRANKLIN WATTS, and associated logos are trademarks and/or registered trademarks of Scholastic Inc.

This book is sold subject to the conditions that it shall not, by way of trade or otherwise, be lent, resold, hired out, or otherwise circulated without the publisher's prior consent in any form or binding or cover other than that in which it is published and without similar condition being imposed on the subsequent purchaser.

You Wouldn't Want to Live Without™

Vegetables!

Written by
Alex Woolf

Illustrated by
David Antram

Series created by
David Salariya

Franklin Watts®
An Imprint of Scholastic Inc.

Contents

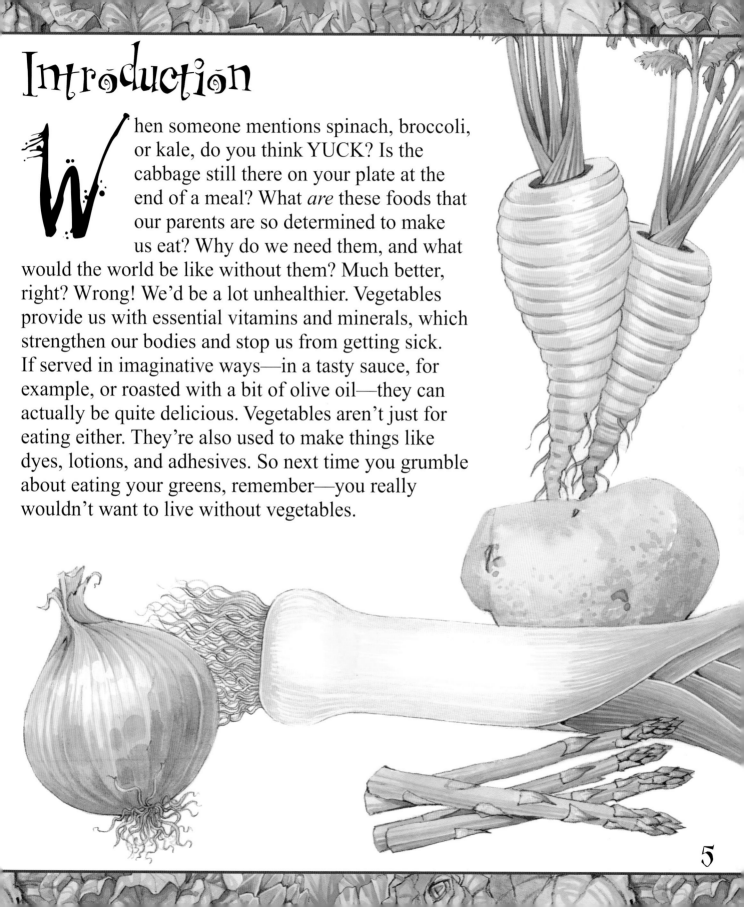

Introduction

When someone mentions spinach, broccoli, or kale, do you think YUCK? Is the cabbage still there on your plate at the end of a meal? What *are* these foods that our parents are so determined to make us eat? Why do we need them, and what would the world be like without them? Much better, right? Wrong! We'd be a lot unhealthier. Vegetables provide us with essential vitamins and minerals, which strengthen our bodies and stop us from getting sick. If served in imaginative ways—in a tasty sauce, for example, or roasted with a bit of olive oil—they can actually be quite delicious. Vegetables aren't just for eating either. They're also used to make things like dyes, lotions, and adhesives. So next time you grumble about eating your greens, remember—you really wouldn't want to live without vegetables.

What Is a Vegetable?

This is actually quite a hard question to answer. If you think you know your onions, here's a test for you. Which of the following foods are vegetables: eggplants, avocados, zucchinis, cucumbers, peas, pumpkins, tomatoes? The answer is none of them are! They're all fruits. It's confusing because in everyday language we call these foods vegetables, yet the strict definition of a vegetable is a seedless, edible part of a plant. All the above foods have seeds, which is why they're fruits. Carrots, onions, cabbages, and potatoes are among the foods that are true vegetables.

I declare you a vegetable!

But...!

TOMATO IN COURT. In 1883, the U.S. Supreme Court ruled that a tomato was a vegetable, not a fruit, because it was eaten as a main course, not as dessert.

THE MUSHROOM is neither a fruit nor a vegetable—it's a fungus, which isn't even a member of the plant kingdom.

I don't know who I am anymore.

I'm actually more closely related to animals than plants.

VEGETABLE PARTS. Most plants have roots, a stem, leaves, flowers, and fruits. The vegetables we eat can be any of the first four of these.

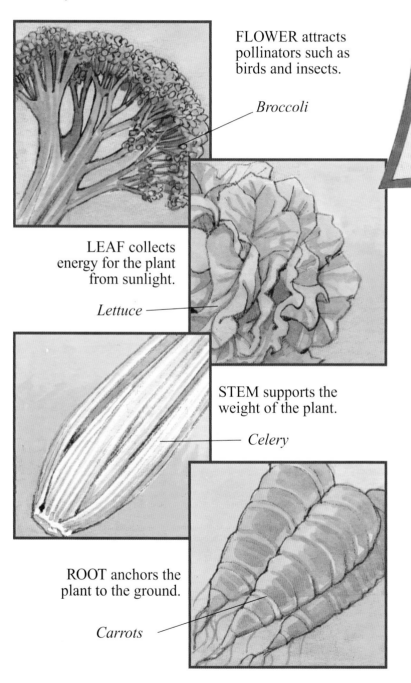

FLOWER attracts pollinators such as birds and insects.

Broccoli

LEAF collects energy for the plant from sunlight.

Lettuce

STEM supports the weight of the plant.

Celery

ROOT anchors the plant to the ground.

Carrots

You Can Do It!

Can you figure out whether the following are fruits or vegetables? Celery, corn, peppers, radishes, spinach, squashes, rhubarb.

Answer: v, f, f, v, v, f, v

Eat your greens!

SEAWEED, popular in many coastal communities, is an algae, not a plant, so it's not a vegetable. But the "crispy seaweed" often served in Chinese restaurants *is* a vegetable, because it's actually dried, deep-fried cabbage!

How Did We Grow Vegetables in the Past?

Humans originally lived as hunter-gatherers. They hunted animals and ate wild plants. They would try eating the fruit, stems, leaves, flowers, and roots of plants they encountered. Many must have been tried and then discarded because they tasted bad or made people sick. But a few plants proved to be tasty and safe, and these were encouraged to grow in forest clearings. This was how vegetable farming began, between 10,000 and 7000 BCE.

Yuck!

How do you do it, Heracles?

THE ANCIENT GREEKS served veggies as a side dish known as *opson* (relish). A favorite food of the mighty hero Heracles was neither a vegetable nor a fruit. It was mashed beans, which are actually legumes (plant seeds that grow in long pods) but are often thought of as vegetables.

I owe it all to mashed beans!

How It Works

For thousands of years, vegetable farming has followed an annual cycle of preparing the soil, sowing the seeds, tending the crops, and harvesting.

He's faster than boiled asparagus!

It tastes better cooked.

Eat a cabbage leaf, and it will grow another. But dig up a potato, and the whole plant dies.

THE EMPEROR AUGUSTUS had a fondness for asparagus, which he preferred lightly boiled. It inspired his favorite phrase, which he used to describe something fast…

THE ROMAN INVADERS introduced many vegetables to Britain, including garlic, onions, shallots, leeks, cabbages, celery, turnips, and radishes. Leeks were so popular that they later became the national emblem of Wales.

VEGETARIANISM. Many Hindus, Buddhists, and Jains are vegetarians because they don't believe in killing animals for meat. Jains try not to kill any plants either, so they avoid eating root vegetables.

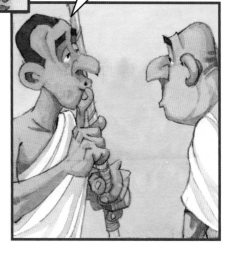

Do Vegetables Make Us Healthy?

Vegetables are an important part of a healthy diet. They are mostly low in fat and contain essential vitamins and minerals. They also supply us with dietary fiber, helping digestion. People who regularly eat vegetables are less likely to suffer from cancer, strokes, and cardiovascular disease (disease of the heart or blood vessels). Most doctors recommend between five and nine servings of fruits and vegetables daily for a healthy diet.

A Balanced Diet

Can this be one of my five-a-day?

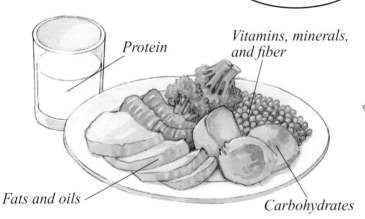

Protein

Vitamins, minerals, and fiber

Fats and oils

Carbohydrates

A BALANCED DIET contains all the nutrients you need to stay healthy and active. The main groups of nutrients are proteins; carbohydrates; fats and oils; and vitamins, minerals, and fiber.

SCURVY, a disease caused by a lack of vitamin C, was once a big problem on sea voyages. In 1768, Captain James Cook discovered that adding vegetables to sailors' diets helped prevent scurvy.

No.

Something in this makes people healthy—but what?

1. Keep vegetables where you can see them, so you're more likely to eat them.
2. Try out new veggies. Variety is healthy.
3. Skip the potatoes and instead eat veggies more packed with vitamins and minerals.

MINERALS. Calcium (broccoli, celery, green onion) fortifies bones and teeth; iron (spinach, Swiss chard, leeks) helps red blood cells; and potassium (all vegetables) helps muscles and nerves, and may prevent high blood pressure.

TOXINS. Some vegetables contain toxins (poisonous substances), which ward off insects and predators that might attack the plant. These can cause stomach ailments if eaten raw, but cooking should destroy any toxins.

DISCOVERY. In the early 1900s, scientists realized that foods such as vegetables provided certain essential nutrients that the body couldn't make by itself. These were called vitamins.

VITAMINS. Vitamin A (carrots, spinach, broccoli) stimulates new cell growth; vitamin B (green vegetables) converts food into energy; and vitamin C (sprouts, cabbage, cauliflower) strengthens the immune system.

11

What Are the Origins of the Onion?

Onions have been adding flavor to meals all over the world for thousands of years. The ancient Egyptians worshipped the onion. They saw it as a symbol of eternity because of its round shape and multiple layers. Onions have been used in many folk remedies. Whatever their medicinal value, they're certainly healthy, being rich in vitamin C and a good source of fiber. They can be eaten raw or cooked. They belong to the *Allium* genus, which also includes garlic, chives, shallots, and leeks.

Place this under your pillow and it will help you sleep.

I know those onions are looking at me!

It will make me run faster!

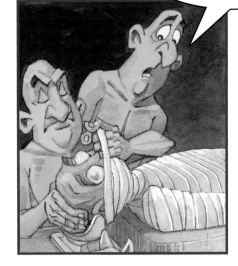

ONION EYES. Ancient Egyptians buried onions with the pharaohs, and even placed them in the mummies' eye sockets!

ATHLETE'S FRIEND. Ancient Greek athletes drank onion juice and rubbed onions on their bodies before competing in the Olympic Games.

How It Works

Onions make you cry when you chop them because they contain chemicals called sulfur compounds. These form into a gas when the onion is chopped, and this irritates the eyes, causing them to tear up.

Just what we always wanted!

Scalpel... Forceps...Onion...

IN MEDIEVAL TIMES, onions not only were eaten, but were used to treat headaches, snakebites, and hair loss. They were valued highly enough to be accepted as a rent payment or even as a wedding gift.

THE ROMANS ate onions regularly, and also used them as a remedy for poor vision, dog bites, mouth sores, toothaches, dysentery, and back pain.

IN COLONIAL AMERICA, Native Americans ate onions both raw and cooked. They used them to make dyes or poultices and their children even played with them as toys.

13

Why Are We Passionate About Potatoes?

French-style potatoes, Mr. President.

Actually, they're Belgian...

FRENCH FRIES. President Thomas Jefferson introduced fries to the U.S. when he had "potatoes served in the French manner" at an 1802 White House dinner. The Belgians claim that they are the real inventors of this dish.

Potatoes are among the most popular food crops in the world. Yet 500 years ago, potatoes were unheard of outside of Peru in South America. The Incas of Peru began growing potatoes between 8000 and 5000 BCE, but it wasn't until 1532 CE, when Spanish conquistadors reached Peru, that Europeans encountered the crop. By the 1570s, Basque sailors were growing them along the coast of northern Spain. Potatoes arrived in the American colonies in 1621. Before long, they had become a staple crop throughout Europe and the New World.

POTATO FAMINE. Potato blight swept across Europe in the1840s, ruining the crops. The Irish suffered the most. Almost a million people died. Another two million left Ireland, mostly for North America.

Hey, these are great!

CHIPS. In 1853, tycoon Cornelius Vanderbilt complained that his potatoes were cut too thick. The angry chef sliced some paper thin. Vanderbilt loved them, and potato chips have been popular ever since.

POTATOES IN SPACE! In October 1995, potatoes became the first vegetable to be grown in space. One day, they may be used to feed astronauts on long space voyages to Mars and beyond.

FRENCH KING Louis XVI (1774–1792) was a big fan of the potato, and he and his wife, Marie Antoinette, did a lot to make it popular in France.

15

When Did We Get Crazy About Carrots?

The sweet, juicy, plump, orange carrot that we know and love today is a fairly recent vegetable, dating back only to the 16th century. Before that, carrots were purple, white, or yellow. They were thin, small, usually forked, and had quite a bitter taste. Temple paintings in Egypt from 2000 BCE show a purple plant that may have been a carrot. The Greeks and Romans grew carrot plants, though only for their seeds and leaves, which they used in their medicines. The Afghans were the first to grow carrot roots for food, in 3000 BCE. The idea of carrots as food reached Asia Minor and Europe between the 8th and 9th centuries. Finally, Dutch growers got to work creating the modern orange carrot.

POISON ANTIDOTE. King Mithradates VI of Pontus (ca.100 BCE) used carrot seeds in a recipe for counteracting poisons—and it worked!

How It Works

Carrots are orange because they contain a pigment called beta-carotene, which is also found in pumpkins, apricots, and nectarines.

Nice color!

HOUSE OF ORANGE. There is a legend that the Dutch bred the orange carrot to honor King William I of the royal House of Orange, but it's probably not a true story.

How are they shooting down our bombers?

Carrots, sir!

WORLD WAR II. British night fighter pilots used onboard radar to shoot down German planes. To keep the technology secret, a myth was spread that the pilots ate carrots to see better in the dark. This is still believed by many today.

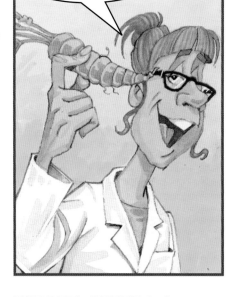

It's the future!

THE BETA SWEET. Is the carrot changing? A group of scientists at Texas A&M University have developed a highly nutritious carrot with purple skin and orange flesh, containing cancer-preventing substances.

What's the Low-Down on Lettuce?

Lettuce is the most popular of the salad vegetables and has been grown since ancient Egyptian times. But the lettuce of those days was a very different crop, with a long stem that was eaten like celery. Over the centuries, the Egyptians bred lettuce with broader, edible leaves. This type was known as romaine. Later, other forms of lettuce appeared, including Boston (small, with soft, oily leaves) and iceberg (with a large, firm head).

MILKY PLANT. The name "lettuce" comes from the Latin *lactis*, meaning milk, because of the milky sap, called latex, found in the stems and branches of lettuce plants.

SLEEPY SALAD. The ancient Romans believed that lettuce made people sleepy, so Emperor Domitian served it at the start of his feasts. He wanted to torment his guests by forcing them to stay awake in his presence.

Hmm...The leaves aren't bad.

Top Tip

Lettuce is one of the few vegetables that you have to eat fresh. You can't freeze, can, dry, or pickle it. The best place to store lettuce is in the crisper drawer of your refrigerator.

This is all we have.

Okay, let's put it together and see what we get.

CAESAR SALAD. In 1924, restaurateur Caesar Cardini invented a new salad using romaine lettuce, croutons, and Parmesan cheese. Caesar salad became popular and renewed people's interest in lettuce.

ICEBERG. In the 1930s, to keep lettuce fresh during transportation across the U.S., it was covered with ice. As the train pulled into each stop, people would call out: "The icebergs are coming!" That's how iceberg lettuce got its name.

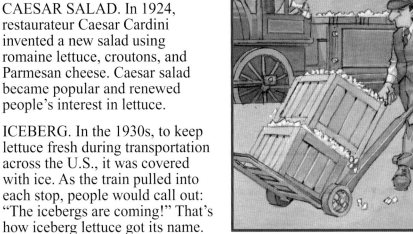

19

Why Are We Captivated by Cabbage?

Ugh! Boiled cabbage! There must be poor people around.

Cabbage, from the French *caboche,* meaning "head," has been grown for thousands of years. Loved by the ancient Greeks and Romans, it was spread throughout northern Europe by the conquering armies of Julius Caesar. Not only did they use cabbage for food, they also covered wounds with its leaves to reduce swelling. The popularity of cabbage spread among the peasantry during the Middle Ages, because it was so easy to grow.

DIOGENES, the Greek philosopher, advised a wealthy courtier: "If you lived on cabbage, you would not need to flatter the powerful." The courtier saw things the other way around.

If you flattered the powerful, you wouldn't need to live on cabbage!

VILE VEGETABLE. The nobility was suspicious of cabbage, which was rumored to cause the plague (it didn't). Many found the strong aroma of boiling cabbage offensive. Yet for the peasants it was a highly nutritious food, full of vitamin C, minerals, and fiber.

Cabbage grows best in rich, moist soil. Grow the seeds indoors for 8 to 10 weeks before transplanting them to the garden. Although cabbage plants thrive in cool weather, frost can damage the young transplants, so check the weather reports first.

If this doesn't work, we'll have to cut your leg off.

CABBAGE AT SEA. Captain James Cook took cabbage with him on his 1768 voyage. It helped his crew avoid not only scurvy, but also gangrene—the ship's doctor applied cabbage-leaf poultices to their wounds.

THE CABBAGE FAMILY includes cauliflower and broccoli. Italian noblewoman Catherine de Medici may have introduced broccoli to France when she married Henry II in 1533.

Are Vegetables Just for Eating?

Vegetables are not just food. They are used in many other ways, both in factories and in homes. Potato starch, for example, is used in many different products, from packing material to glue. Lettuce sap has been used as a folk medicine for hundreds of years, treating people for coughs, anxiety, tension, pain, and rheumatism (swollen, painful joints or muscles). You can rub an onion on insect bites or stings to ease the itchiness and pain. Vegetables can be a form of art, sculpted into imaginative shapes, from flowers to jack-o'-lanterns.

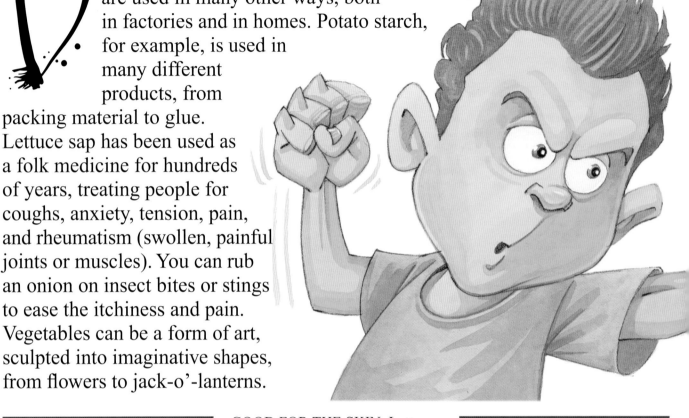

You smell like salad!

GOOD FOR THE SKIN. Lettuce can be used to relieve skin rashes. Today it is used as an ingredient in some soaps and skin lotions.

POLISHING METAL. Slice an onion and then crush it. Mix the crushed onion with water, then use a cloth to rub the mixture onto a metal surface. It will make silverware gleam.

If you have a splinter that you can't remove, tape a piece of raw onion to it and leave it there for about an hour. The anti-inflammatory properties in the onion will draw the splinter to the skin's surface.

You can't hurt me!

VEGETABLE DYES. Vegetables contain chemicals called polyphenols, which attach to fabric and dye it. That's why food can stain your clothes.

BEETS for red or pink dye

ONIONS for yellow or brown dye

SPINACH for green dye

POTATO PLATES! Potato starch is frequently used as an eco-friendly, biodegradable form of plastic, used to make disposable plates, dishes, and silverware.

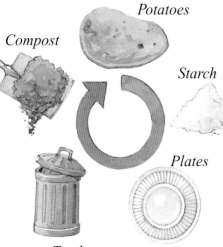

Compost

Potatoes

Starch

Plates

Trash

VEGETABLE CARVING may have begun in ancient China or Japan. Today, carved vegetables are often used as a garnish when serving food. Carrots, radishes, and shallots are great for carving.

How Are Vegetables Grown and Preserved?

For thousands of years, vegetables were grown on small plots of land. They had to be eaten fresh, so any excess had to be sold quickly in nearby towns. The last two centuries have seen big advances in cultivation techniques. The use of better fertilizers, greenhouses, hoop houses, and hydroponics have greatly increased yields, while advances in refrigeration technology have allowed growers to store their produce for longer. They can now grow large quantities of vegetables and sell them in bulk to towns and cities.

From Seed to Stomach

Plow the land

Sow the seeds

Water the plants

Sell the vegetables

Eat the vegetables

Harvest the vegetables

Hydroponics is a way of growing vegetables without soil. They are grown indoors in water rich in mineral nutrients. The crops are better protected from weeds, weather, pests, and diseases, but the yield is lower and more technical knowledge is needed.

GREENHOUSE. The glass traps the Sun's heat, keeping the greenhouse warm, so vegetables can be grown even in the winter.

RAISED-BED GARDENING. Vegetables are grown close together in raised beds enclosed by a frame. The soil is enriched with compost. The closeness of the plants prevents weed growth and conserves moisture.

STORING. After a vegetable is harvested, it starts to lose moisture and vitamin C. Green leafy vegetables wilt quickly if not refrigerated. Root crops, like onions and potatoes, last longer.

PRESERVING. We can preserve vegetables by destroying germs or preventing their growth. This is often done by canning, freezing, pickling in vinegar, or boiling in sugar to create jams.

Do Vegetables Affect the Environment?

Eating vegetables doesn't only make us healthier, it also helps the planet. Vegetable farming uses up fewer natural resources than meat farming and causes less environmental damage. If we all ate less meat and more vegetables, it would reduce global warming: Around 20 percent of all greenhouse gases, like methane, come from livestock farming. Eating less meat would also reduce the amount of land and water needed for farming, so fewer forests would need to be destroyed for cattle grazing.

WATER. It takes a whopping 1,847 gallons (6,992 liters) of water to produce a pound of beef. That includes the water needed to grow the grass and other food for the cow, plus water for drinking and cleaning. Compare that to vegetables, shown here.

garlic: 71 gallons (269 L) per pound

artichokes: 98 gallons (371 L) per pound

lettuce: 28 gallons (106 L) per pound

asparagus: 258 gallons (977 L) per pound

broccoli: 34 gallons (129 L) per pound

It takes 16 pounds of grain to make just one pound of beef.

You Can Do It!

Why not try growing your own vegetables?
• It could save you money
• Gardening is a great form of exercise
• It will help you get your five daily portions of fruit and vegetables

MANY FARMERS use chemical pesticides and fertilizers on their crops. These contain nitrates, which leach into the ground and local waterways. Organic farmers avoid these chemicals.

This came from my garden.

LAND. A vegetarian family needs around 1 acre (0.4 hectare) of land to produce all the food it needs. The average, meat-eating modern family needs 20 acres (8 ha). That's partly because most of our plant crops are consumed by livestock.

I've got a lot more land than you.

You need it.

FOOD MILES. Many supermarket vegetables are imported from distant countries on ships, planes, and trucks, all of which pollute the atmosphere. That's why it's better to buy locally produced vegetables.

These come from the other side of the world.

27

What Happens to Vegetables?

egetables end up in our stomachs. Once our bodies have absorbed their nutrients, we get rid of what we can't digest when we go to the bathroom. Our waste goes through the sewage system to a treatment plant where it is cleaned, sterilized, and then returned to the environment. Some of this sterilized waste, or sludge, is sold to farmers to fertilize soil. It may be used to grow more vegetables. So next time you don't want to eat your vegetables, remember how important they are for your health, and what an important part you play in helping them grow.

> What are you doing in there?

> Playing my part in nature's cycle.

> It's disgusting!

> It's natural.

DECAY. Vegetables are living organisms, and they contain bacteria and fungi. These feed on the vegetables, causing them to spoil. Fungus appears as mold on the food's surface.

To reduce food waste, don't store broccoli, cauliflower, or leafy greens next to apples, apricots, melons, or figs. These fruits emit a gas called ethylene, which makes the vegetables decay faster.

FOOD POISONING. Microbes release chemicals that lower the vegetable's nutritional value. They may also release waste products that can make us sick, which is why we shouldn't eat vegetables that are going bad.

If it's still firm, it's safe to eat after you've removed the sprouts.

Seed starting to sprout

SPROUTED POTATOES. Potatoes are a thick part of the plant's root, called a tuber, and they contain buds. When exposed to light or warmth, the buds can grow into sprouts, or "eyes."

HUMUS. Many vegetables are thrown away uneaten, or never harvested. These decompose naturally, eaten by microbes in the earth to create a dark substance called humus that enriches the soil and makes it fertile.

29

Glossary

Bacteria A group of microorganisms, some of which can cause disease.

Biodegradable Capable of being decomposed by bacteria or other organisms.

Blight A plant disease, especially one caused by a fungus.

Compost Decayed organic material used as plant fertilizer.

Crisper drawer A compartment at the bottom of the refrigerator for storing fruit and vegetables.

Cultivate To raise or grow crops in order to sell them.

Dietary fiber Substances in food, such as cellulose and lignin, which help in the digestive process.

Dysentery A disease of the intestines resulting in severe diarrhea.

Eco-friendly Not harmful to the environment.

Emission The production and discharge of a gas.

Fertilizer A substance added to soil to make it more fertile (capable of producing more crops).

Fungus A family of organisms, including mushrooms, toadstools, molds, and yeasts, that feed on organic matter.

Gangrene The death and decay of tissues in a part of the body.

Genus A group of plants or animals that all have similar characteristics.

Greenhouse gases Gases, such as carbon dioxide, that contribute to the greenhouse effect—the trapping of the Sun's heat in the atmosphere.

Hoop house A long, polythene-covered frame under which seedlings or other plants are grown outdoors.

Immune system The organs and processes of the body that provide resistance to infection.

Livestock Farm animals.

Microbe A microorganism, such as a disease-causing bacterium.

Mineral A solid, inorganic (not carbon-based) natural substance.

Nitrates Chemicals used as fertilizer: sodium nitrate, potassium nitrate, or ammonium nitrate.

Nutrient A substance that provides nourishment essential for growth and a healthy life.

Organic Relating to or obtained from living matter. Organic farming is farming without the use of chemical fertilizers or pesticides.

Pesticide A substance used to destroy insects or other organisms that can be harmful to crops.

Pickle To preserve fruit or vegetables using sugar, vinegar, and brine.

Pigment A substance in animal or plant tissue that gives it its color.

Pollinator Something that deposits pollen on a plant, allowing fertilization.

Poultice A soft, moist material, often from a plant, applied to wounds or infected areas to relieve soreness and inflammation.

Radar A system for detecting the presence, direction, distance, and speed of aircraft and other objects.

Staple crop The main or most important crop.

Starch A substance obtained from foods like potatoes and cereals that contains carbohydrates and is an important part of the human diet.

Vitamin Any of a group of organic chemicals that are essential for growth and nutrition.

Yield The amount of something, such as crops, that are produced.

Index

Top Biggest Vegetables

Cabbage: 138 pounds (62.71 kilograms) Grown by John Evans, U.S., 2012

Sweet potato: 81.5 pounds (37 kg) Grown by Manuel Pérez Pérez, Spain, 2004

Beet: 51.5 pounds (23.4 kg) Grown by Ian Neale, UK, 2001

Broccoli: 34.8 pounds (15.8 kg) Grown by John Evans, U.S., 1993

Cauliflower: 60.6 pounds (27.5 kg) Grown by Peter Glazebrook, UK, 2014

Carrot: 20 pounds (9.1 kg) Grown by Peter Glazebrook, UK, 2014

Onion: 18.7 pounds (8.5 kg) Grown by Tony Glover, UK, 2014

Potato: 11 pounds (4.9 kg) Grown by Peter Glazebrook, UK, 2011

Vegetable carving

No one knows for sure when or where the art of vegetable carving began. Some say it started in 7th-century China. Emperor Zhong Zong wanted to thank the gods for his victory over his enemies, so he asked his cooks to carve mythical animal shapes out of vegetables.

Many people believe this art form first started in Japan, where it is known as mukimono. In ancient Japan, food was served on rough, unglazed plates, and chefs tried to improve the presentation of their dishes by adding an artistically cut or folded salad leaf as a garnish. By the 16th century, the art of mukimono had become part of every chef's training.

According to yet another theory, vegetable carving started in 14th-century Thailand during the Loi Krathong festival when decorated rafts were paraded through the streets. Nang Noppamart, a servant to the king, decided to carve a flower and a bird from a vegetable for her raft. The king was so impressed, he decreed that from then on, every woman should learn this new art form.

Whatever its origins, vegetable carving flourishes to this day, and not just in Asia. Throughout the world, people are experimenting with carving carrots, radishes and shallots into exquisitely intricate and delicate shapes.

Did You Know?

- It is actually possible to turn your skin a shade of orange by eating too many orange carrots.

- For the Incas, a unit of time was based on how long it took to cook a potato.

- Coleslaw, the cabbage-based salad, is based on the Danish words *kool*, meaning "cabbage," and *sla*, meaning "salad."

- According to legend, Drusus (13 BCE–23 CE), son of Roman Emperor Tiberius, loved broccoli so much that he gorged himself on it, eating nothing else for an entire month. His urine turned bright green.

- Fossil pollen dating from the Eocene period (56–34 million years ago) has been identified as belonging to the carrot family.

- Although most scholars believe the modern orange carrot wasn't developed until the 17th century, there is an illustration of one in a Byzantine book dated 512 CE. Maybe there was an earlier version of the orange carrot?

- Potatoes are a member of the nightshade family, which includes the poisonous belladonna plant.

- Most people know that New York's nickname is The Big Apple. Fewer people know that Chicago's name comes from the French version of a Native American word that means "Stinky Onion."

- According to folklore, the thicker an onion's skin, the more severe the coming winter is likely to be.